Famous Places

Bernadette Kelly

Contents

Around the World

Hi, I'm Karl.

Have you ever wanted to see the most famous places in the world?

Throughout history, people have built amazing things on every **continent**.

Let's take a look at some of them!

ITALY
UNITED STATES
OF AMERICA
CHINA
EGYPT
PERU
AUSTRALIA

Sydney Harbour

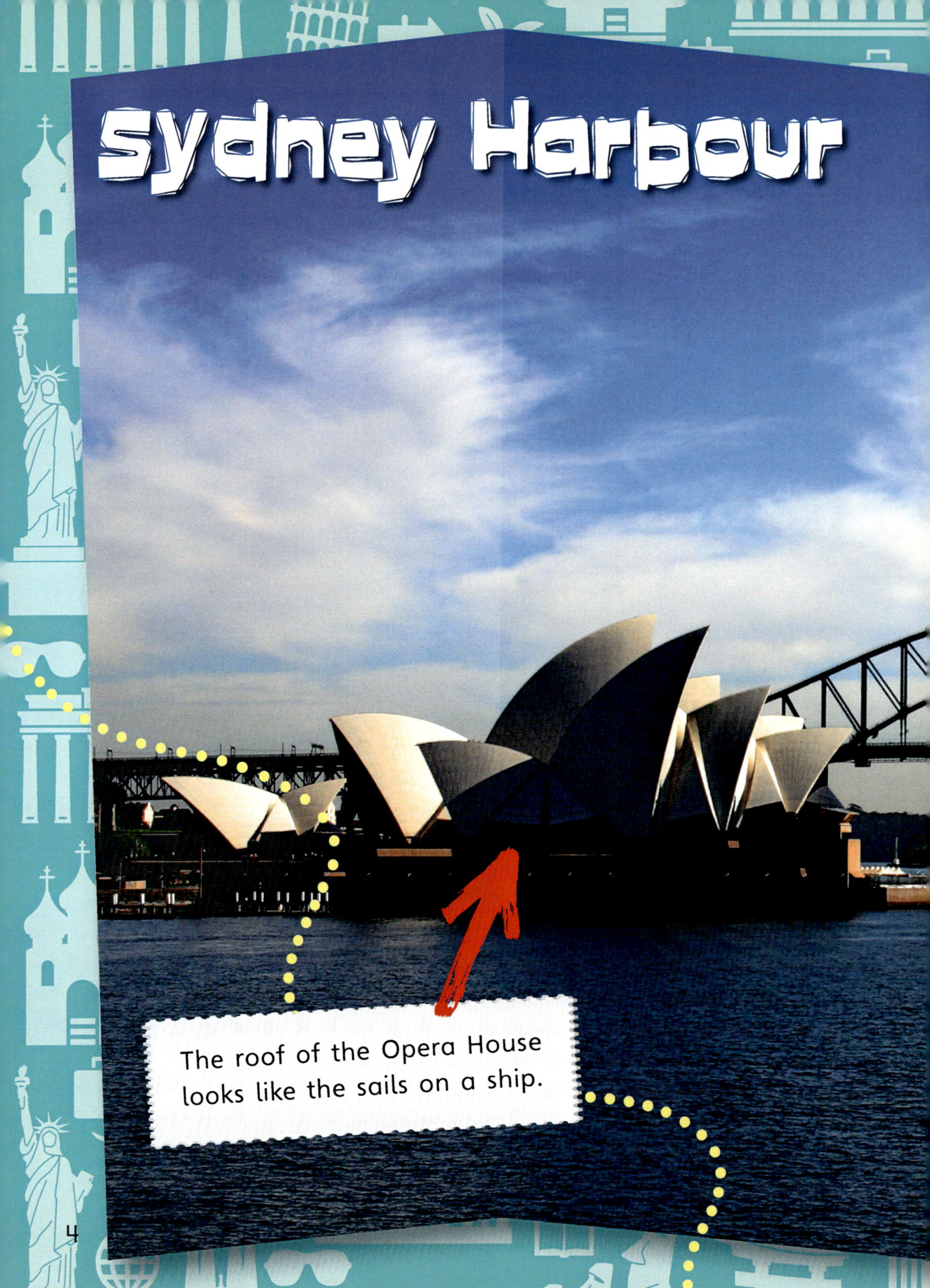

The roof of the Opera House looks like the sails on a ship.

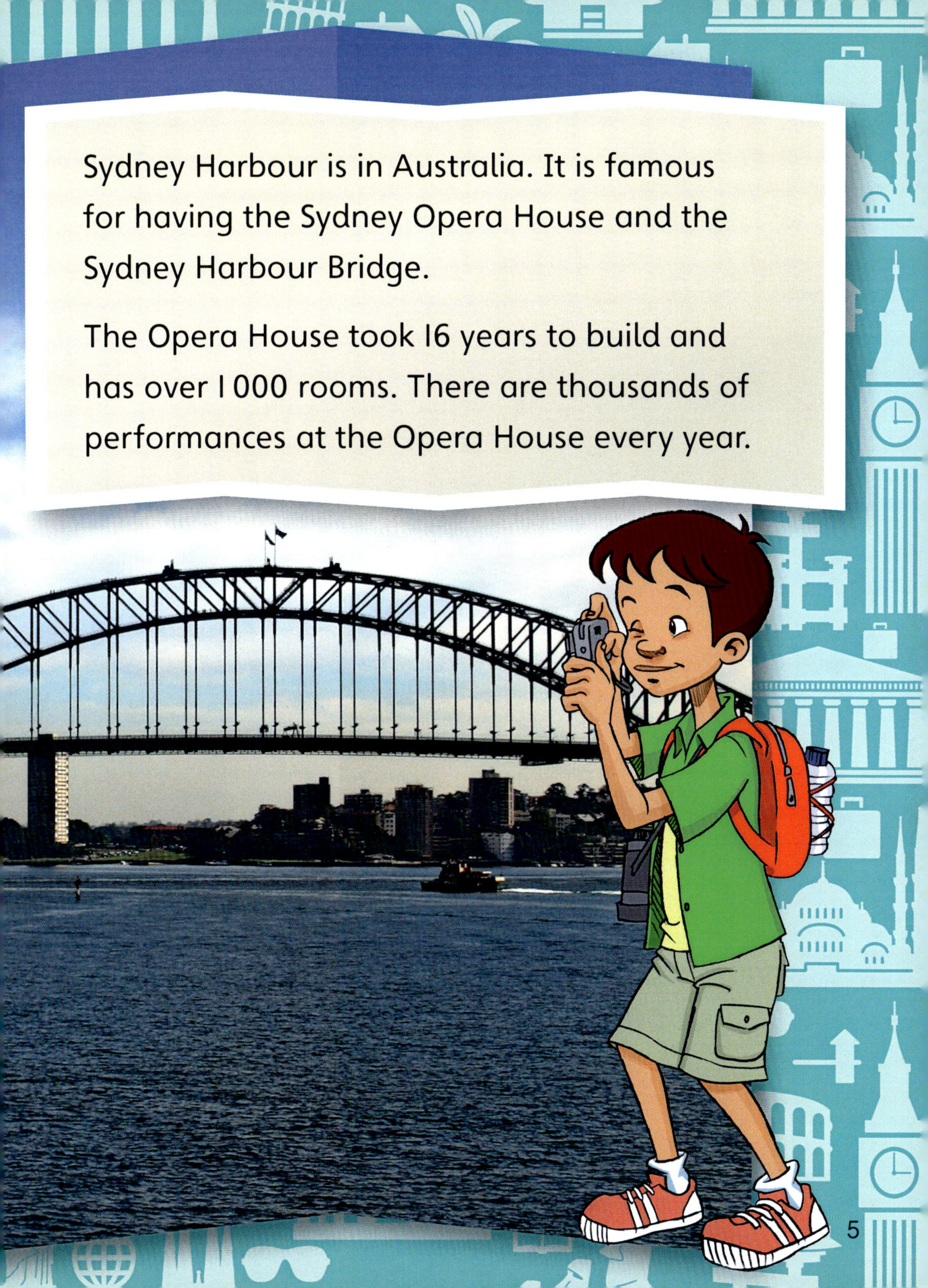

Sydney Harbour is in Australia. It is famous for having the Sydney Opera House and the Sydney Harbour Bridge.

The Opera House took 16 years to build and has over 1 000 rooms. There are thousands of performances at the Opera House every year.

Every day, hundreds of people climb the Sydney Harbour Bridge.

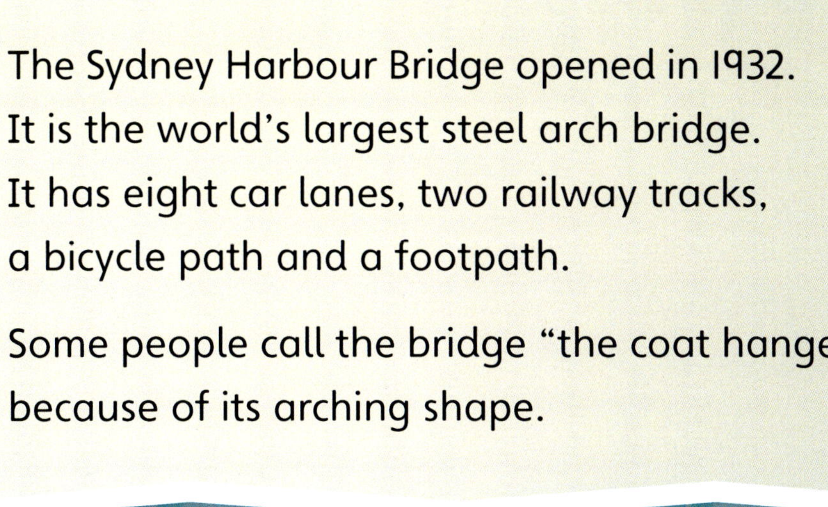

The Sydney Harbour Bridge opened in 1932. It is the world's largest steel arch bridge. It has eight car lanes, two railway tracks, a bicycle path and a footpath.

Some people call the bridge "the coat hanger" because of its arching shape.

STAGE 1

STAGE 2

STAGE 3

STAGE 4

STAGE 5

It took 8 years to build the Sydney Harbour Bridge.

The Great Wall of China

Many people think that the wall can be seen from the Moon, but this is not true.

The Great Wall of China is the longest wall ever built. More than one million workers and soldiers built the wall.

The Great Wall of China is not just one long wall. It is a collection of shorter sections of wall. Chinese **emperors** added new sections to the wall over many thousands of years.

The Great Wall was built to keep out China's enemies.

The Great Pyramid of Giza

The Great Pyramid of Giza is the largest pyramid in Egypt. It was built 4 500 years ago as a burial tomb for a **pharaoh**. There are many tunnels and tombs inside the pyramid.

Ancient writing called hieroglyphics (say *hire-oh-gliff-iks*) can be seen on the walls inside the pyramid.

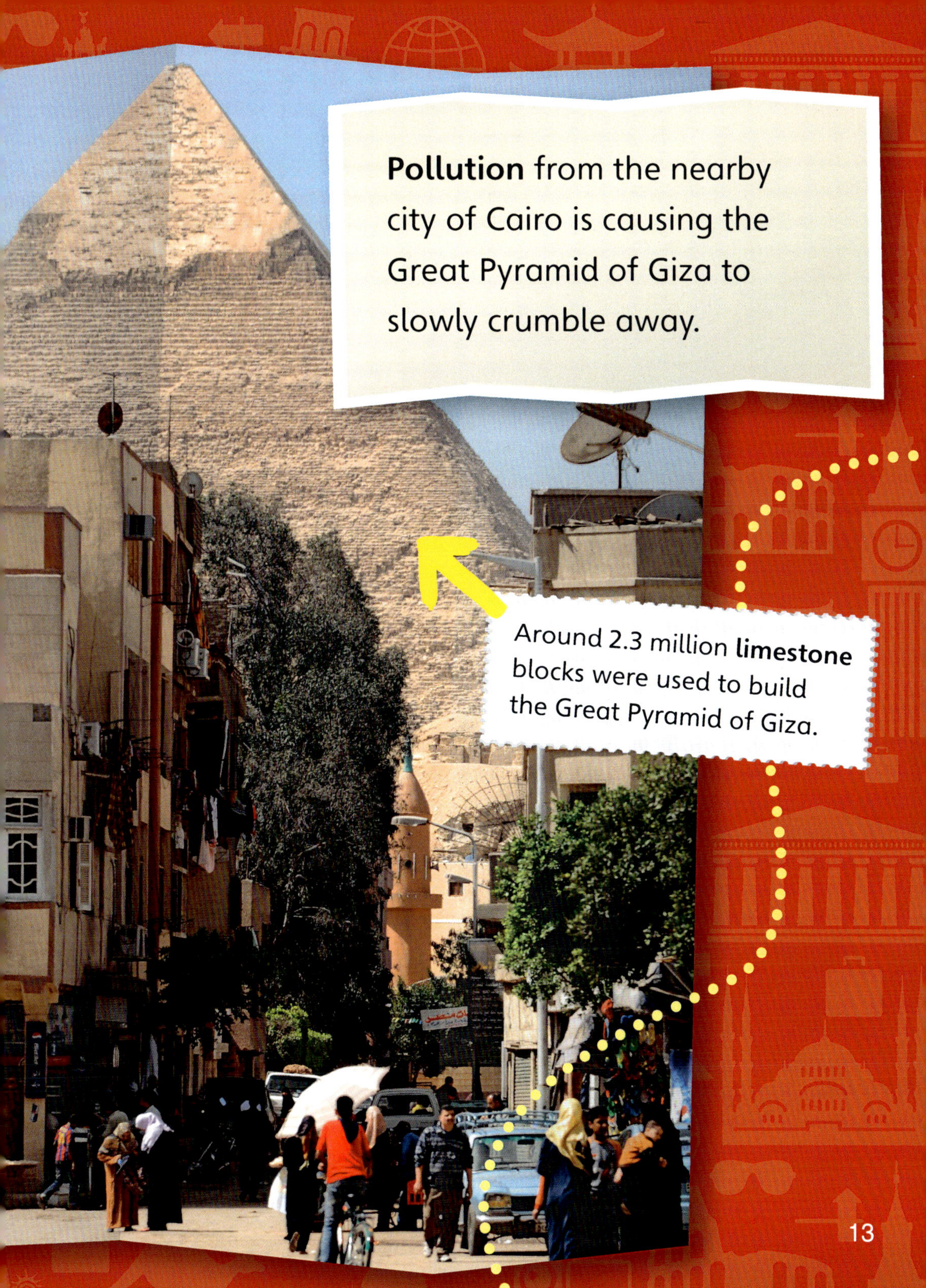

Pollution from the nearby city of Cairo is causing the Great Pyramid of Giza to slowly crumble away.

Around 2.3 million **limestone** blocks were used to build the Great Pyramid of Giza.

The Great Sphinx is
73.5 metres long.
It originally had a
long braided beard
and a nose, but they
are now gone.

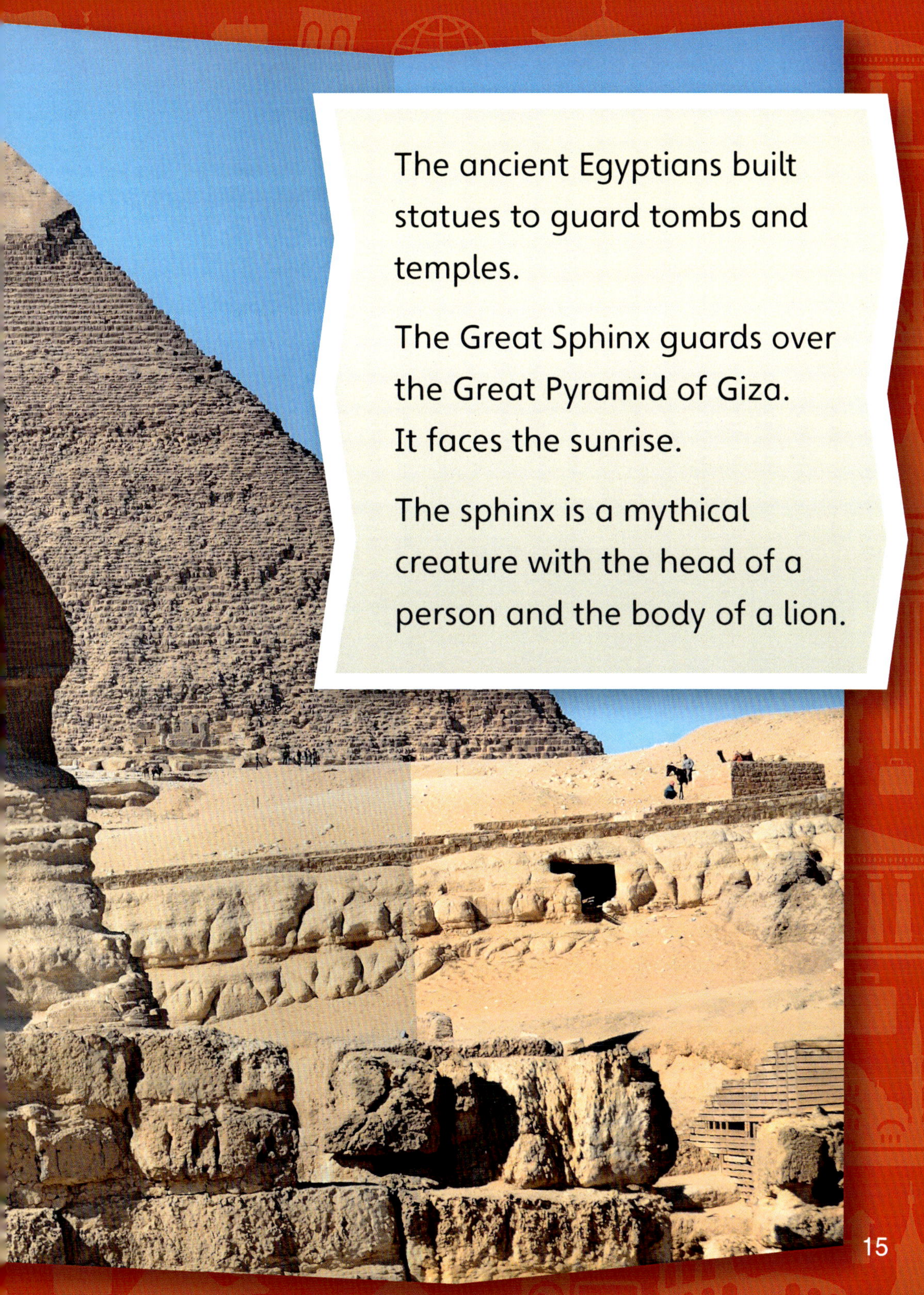

The ancient Egyptians built statues to guard tombs and temples.

The Great Sphinx guards over the Great Pyramid of Giza. It faces the sunrise.

The sphinx is a mythical creature with the head of a person and the body of a lion.

The Leaning Tower of Pisa

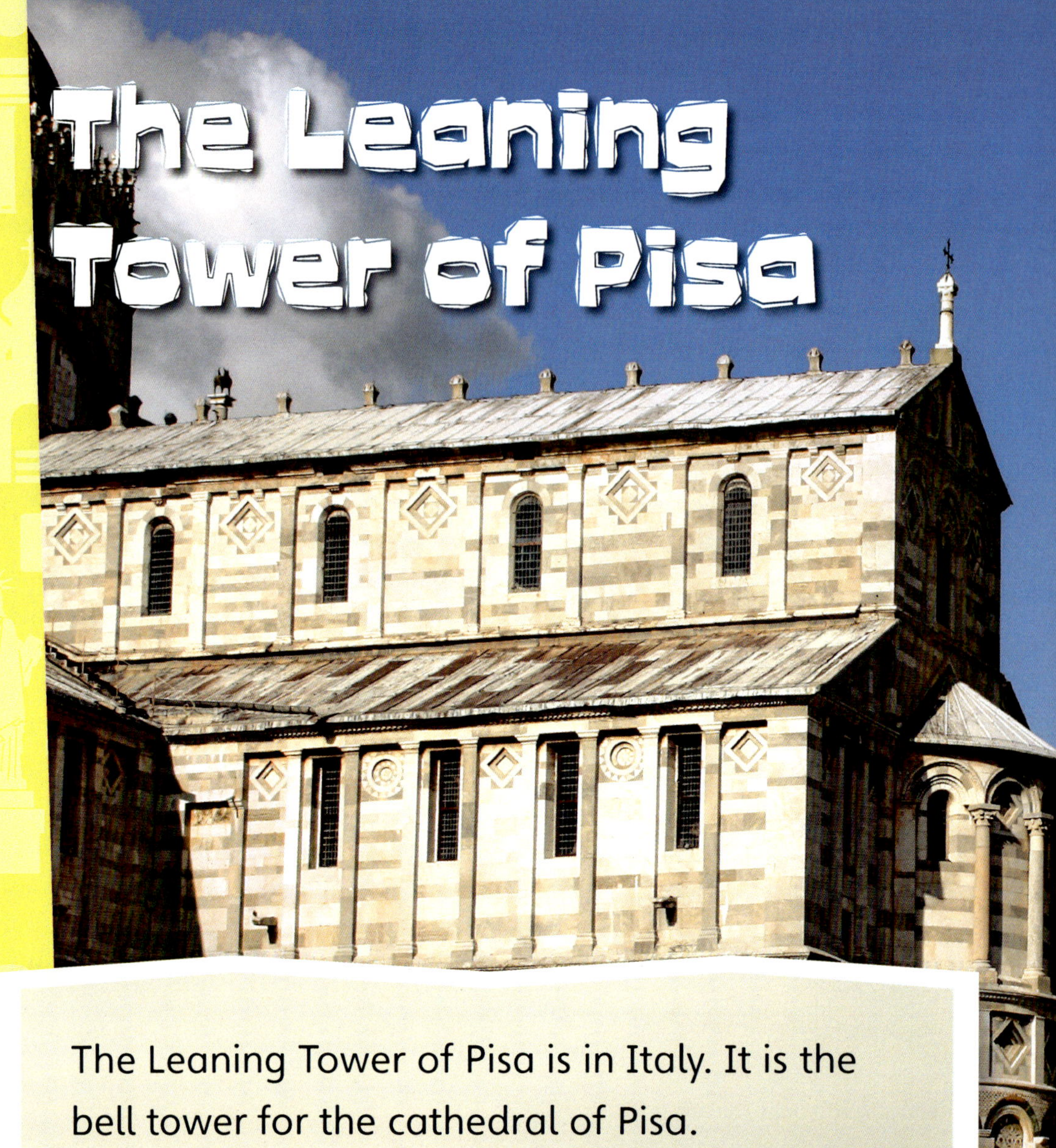

The Leaning Tower of Pisa is in Italy. It is the bell tower for the cathedral of Pisa.

It leans to the side because it was built on soft ground. The **foundation** was also too small for the weight it had to support.

Thousands of tourists visit the Leaning Tower of Pisa to take photos like this!

People worked for many years to straighten the tower.

The third floor of the tower was built before the lean was noticed. After that, construction stopped for 100 years in the hope that the ground would settle over time. When the building of the tower began again, it still leaned.

Today, the tower has been made stronger to stop it from falling down.

Mount Rushmore

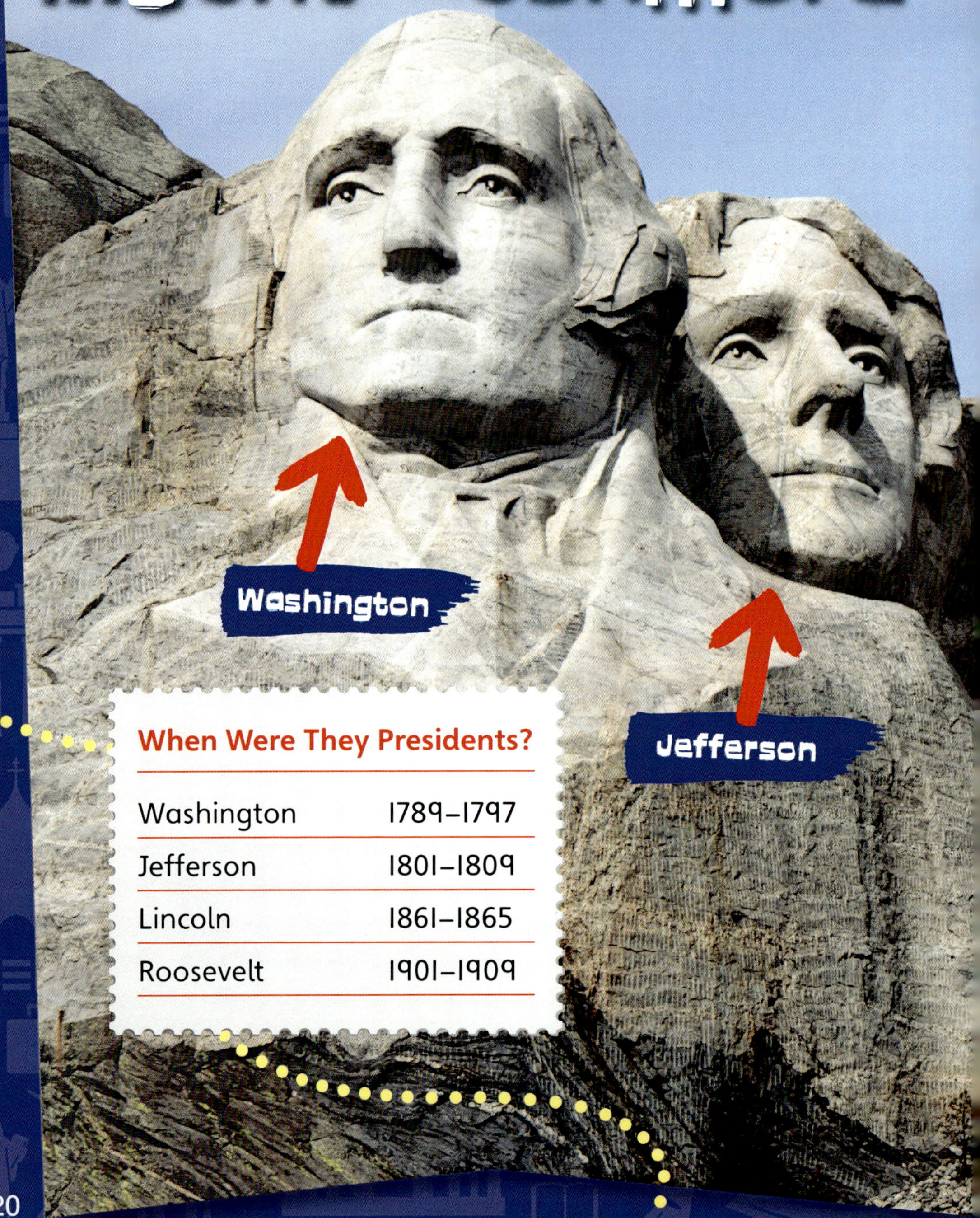

Washington

Jefferson

When Were They Presidents?

Washington	1789–1797
Jefferson	1801–1809
Lincoln	1861–1865
Roosevelt	1901–1909

Mount Rushmore is in South Dakota, in the United States of America. The heads of four American presidents have been carved into the rock on the mountain. The presidents are George Washington, Thomas Jefferson, Theodore Roosevelt and Abraham Lincoln.

The carvings on Mount Rushmore took 14 years to complete. Over 450 000 kilograms of stone was removed from Mount Rushmore during that time.

At first, Thomas Jefferson's face was on George Washington's right side, but it was blasted off and put on to his left side because the rock was weak in that area.

Each head is as tall as
a six-storey building.
6th storey
5th storey
4th storey
3rd storey
2nd storey
1st storey

Machu Picchu

Machu Picchu (say *Mah-choo Peek-choo*) is an ancient city that sits high in the Andes Mountains in Peru. The **Incas** built the city in the 15th century.

For a long time, the city was not used. It became covered in plants and trees. A professor found the city again in 1911.

Machu Picchu may have been built as the home for an emperor.

Many of the buildings have now been restored to show people how they would have looked in Inca times.

Thousands of tourists visit Machu Picchu each year. The best way to get to Machu Picchu is to take a train or walk along the Inca trail.

In Spanish, the meaning of the name Machu Picchu is "old mountain".

Where to Next?

Statue of Liberty

Taj Mahal

Now you have seen some of the amazing things that people have built around the world, can you think of any others?

What famous places would you like to visit next?

Eiffel Tower
Big Ben
Stonehenge

Famous Places Quiz

How much do you remember? Can you work out which famous places are in these photos?

Answers: I Machu Picchu, **2** The Great Sphinx **3** The Sydney Harbour Bridge, **4** The Great Wall of China, **5** Mount Rushmore, **6** The Leaning Tower of Pisa, **7** The Great Pyramid of Giza, **8** The Sydney Opera House

Glossary

ancient	having existed for many years
centuries	one century is one hundred years
continent	large area of land: Antarctica, Asia, Africa, Australia, Europe, North America, South America
emperors	kings
foundation	the bottom part of a building that supports the whole building
Incas	South American Indigenous people
limestone	a hard rock, used for building
pharaoh	Egyptian king
pollution	when harmful substances come into the environment